OLD DOLLS

BY

ELEANOR ST. GEORGE

GRAMERCY PUBLISHING COMPANY
NEW YORK

FOREWORD

To each of us one particular hobby is the most fascinating, and so it is with dolls, whether dollmaking or doll collecting. In the more than forty years that I have been professionally interested in dolls I have "serviced" and helped to build most of the well-known collections in America. I have made two long tours through the country to visit every collection within reach. I never saw two that were much alike: for some collectors only age matters; others care only for beauty. Then there are those who demand both age and beauty, and I saw a few outstanding collections that included the whole field—prehistoric dolls to the latest creations of New York and Hollywood.

Why is this hobby of dolls spreading so fast and taking so firm a hold? Perhaps because the love of dolls is basic. Dolls, little manikins, appear in man's earliest artistic efforts. Of the very old ones only those of stone and clay survive, and it is doubtful if these were ever toys.

Today, some thirty years since doll collecting began, there are several interesting books on the subject, among them Eleanor St. George's first one *The Dolls of Yesterday*. Her research has been thorough and she has proved herself equipped, as student and collector, to deal with the subject. Much remains to be discovered about old dolls, especially the ceramic types. Information on these will come from old factory sites in Europe which now await investigation. Perhaps this wonderful little introductory book on dolls will inspire someone who has means and time for this fascinating research. Undoubtedly *Old Dolls* will be warmly received, for Eleanor St. George, with knowledge and enthusiasm covers in this small space the whole delightful subject of dolls in a way to inspire new collectors and to extend the information of the old.

Emma C. Clear

Humpty Dumpty Doll Hospital,
Redondo Beach, California,
December 26, 1949

CONTENTS

TO CHARLES,

the most understanding of collectors' husbands

PREFACE

This book is not intended to be an exhaustive treatment of the subject of old dolls. There are many types not even mentioned, such as certain rare dolls, which are for the advanced collector. It is our intention merely to give beginners information on the possibilities of the hobby, and the fun to be had. As you advance in knowledge and become wiser as to where to find dolls and what to pay for them, you can learn further about them in more extensive books on the subject. New books are constantly being written as information on old dolls comes to light.

It is a pity that for so many generations dolls were regarded merely as toys and carelessly handled. The wonder is that so many have come down to us intact. Knowledge of makers, place of manufacture, and other information we should like to have, has passed into oblivion.

The hobby of doll collecting—with few exceptions—is only about thirty years old. Yet there are upwards of ten thousand collectors in the United States, and a friend, recently returned from Europe, says that dolls—and buttons too— are as much in demand abroad as they are here.

It is interesting to see the way "hobby fevers" spread.

Before collecting began, dolls were little valued, even in antique shops. In the writer's collection is a lovely Empress Eugenie doll-head, trimmed with luster, but it cost only twenty-five cents. This Parian treasure came from a shop run by an old Quaker Negro on Pine Street in Philadelphia. It stood among luster pitchers for some twenty years. Then a body was put on and the doll was dressed. Today its value runs to three figures.

ELEANOR ST. GEORGE

Sybilholme,
Quechee, Vermont,
January, 1950

I. PEDDLER DOLLS

The collecting of old dolls is one of the most delightful of modern hobbies, not only because of the beauty and variety of the dolls themselves, but because of the bypaths of history, biography, literature, manners and customs, superstitions and folklore, sentiment and memory down which collecting leads. Dolls are almost as old as the human race. In Japan, they appear in pictures that were doubtless painted more than two thousand years ago. They have been found in the tombs of Egypt, Greece, and Rome.

Dolls have been made of many materials: ivory, bone, wood, canvas stuffed with papyrus, rags, papier-mâché, china, Parian (which is a soft, white china, unglazed and resembling marble), bisque, composition, clay, shells, sponges, wax, apples, nuts, beads, rubber, rawhide—to mention a few. Through the ages, dolls have served man in many ways. Among primitive peoples they may first have been idols or household gods; wax dolls were sold outside Christian churches in Italy for votive offerings; wooden dolls clustered around

2. *Rubber-Head Doll. I. R. Comb Co. Twenty-two inches high. Collection of Mrs. Chester Dimick, Gales Ferry, Conn.*

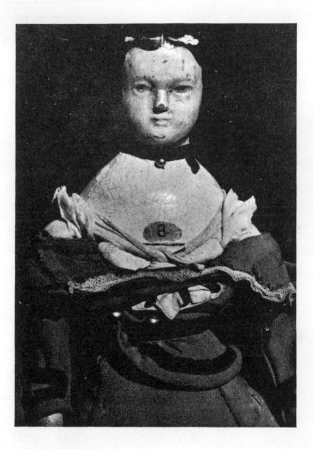

3. Doll with Rawhide Head. F. E. Darrow, Bristol, Conn. Collection of Mrs. Chester Dimick, Gales Ferry, Conn.

the Christmas crèche of the infant Jesus to portray the story of the Nativity.

In very early Japan the puppet show supplied entertainment. In the courts of medieval Europe, dolls were messengers of fashion and before there were such things as colored fashion plates, Milliners' Models were sent from France to England and America to show the new styles. French-fashion dolls were used in the same way in the latter half of the nineteenth century. How many centuries they also served as the beloved toys of children is a matter of conjecture.

The ancient dolls of the Egyptians, Greeks, and Romans are in museums, where they should be, as are most of the wooden and wax dolls of the eighteenth century. A very few dolls of the time of Queen Anne are still to be had, but the collector generally must look for dolls of the nineteenth and twentieth centuries.

The few dolls of the eighteenth century which may still be found are either of wood or wax—mostly wood. Of these the peddler dolls are the most interesting. In the eighteenth century, women traveled about the countryside—as pack-peddlers did a generation ago in this country—selling needles, pins, and other small articles. These women were called Notion Nannies and were familiar figures in English country districts.

The peddler dolls commemorate a social custom. They are of carved wood and usually carry a basket containing numerous miniature articles. Such a doll, from the collection of the Victoria and Albert Museum appears as a frontispiece. Some of these old peddler dolls have found their way to America. Mrs. DeWitt Clinton Cohen of New York has a wonderful collection of them, one of which has 125 articles on the tray. The author owns one that was found for her in northern England during World War II. It dates from 1780 and had been bought by an antique dealer at a farm auction in Nottinghamshire.

A collection of old dolls may often start with a beloved childhood favorite or the venerated relic of a former generation found in a forgotten trunk or chest in an attic—and indeed, there are more such chests still to be investigated than you would suppose. You never know where the next addition to your dolls may come from—an appealing aspect of collecting. When you become doll-conscious, it may be you will discover a valuable china head in the cellar of the oldest house in your town, as did Mrs. Erwin Chapin of Silver Creek, New York. Auctions, antique shops, and Good Will shops are other possible sources. The author even received three wonderful dolls instead of flowers during a hospital stay— a brown-eyed china-head doll, a Jumeau French-bisque, and a fifteen-inch Joel Ellis doll with its original Joel Ellis carriage. You never know!

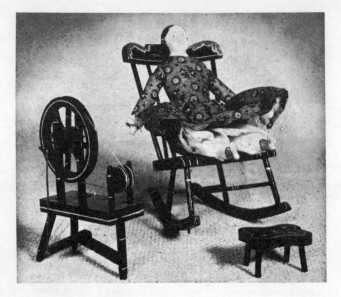

4. China-Head Doll. Found in the oldest house in Silver Creek, N. Y. Collection of Mrs. Erwin Chapin, Silver Creek.

"Is doll collecting expensive?" It may or may not be, as you choose. It just depends on what type you seek. On a modest budget, you may collect paper dolls, penny dolls, or what are now called "Frozen Charlottes," those stiff little jointless bisque and china dolls that we used to call twenty-five-cent dolls. Or you may collect Parians, or French-fashion dolls at top prices. There are many gradations between these. Certainly you may assemble a good general collection at not too great a price. Hardly any collectible material has so increased in value in the last few years as old dolls. Doubtless they will continue to grow in worth for years to come, because the supply is necessarily limited and the number of new collectors grows annually.

II. MILLINERS' MODELS

According to German sources of information, papier-mâché—macerated paper mixed with glue —was first used for doll heads about 1820. It was probably invented by the Italians and was used in other countries for small objects, such as boxes and trays, and for architectural moldings prior to its use for dolls. We do not know who first made the Milliners' Models, those dolls with stiff, unjointed, kid bodies, wooden arms and legs, and papier-mâché heads, with a variety of molded hair styles like those popular from 1820 to about 1860. This seems to be the period during which these dolls were made, but *where* is not known. Some authorities suggest Holland but nobody really knows.

The Milliners' Models vary in size from about five to twenty-six inches. The original dresses were usually white net over pink cambric. Their purpose was, as the name implies, to carry to England and the United States before there were fashion journals—and for quite a long time afterward too—the latest styles in dressmaking and

5. Milliners' Model. An early style, six inches high. Collection of Mrs. William Walker, Louisville, Ky.

hairdressing. These model dolls were apparently imported in considerable numbers. When they had served the commercial world, they found their way into the nursery, whence many of them have come down to us.

Children had few toys in the early days and these little creatures must have seemed very wonderful to them. The author has an early Milliners'-Model doll in her collection that was found in the wall of an old house in Burlington, Vermont. It had crude child-made clothes like those in early prints. Some little girl of long ago must have had a marvelous time with her and loved her well. Perhaps the doll had been put to sleep in a broken place in the wall, and was forgotten and plastered into her hiding place when the hole was repaired. There she had lain for decades, until the house was torn down.

One of the very earliest Milliners' Models, according to the hair styling, is Mrs. William Walker's twenty-six-inch doll, shown here with hair done in three puffs, one on each side of the face and the third at the top. This kind of doll usually comes only in small sizes. The dolls of 1840 and thereabouts wear long curls on their necks; those of the 1850 to 1860 decade are likely to have short curls arranged around the head, like that of the common china-head doll. Occasionally the familiar chignon or waterfall appears with a net such as that of *Miss Amanda*

6. LEFT: *Earliest Milliners' Model. Found in the wall of a house in Burlington, Vt.* RIGHT: Miss Amanda Bandy, *a Milliners' Model. St. George Collection*

7. *Papier-mâché Dolls with Wigs. Unusual. The lady has "flirting" eyes. Collection of Edna Fletcher, Newburgh, N. Y.*

Bandy in the writer's collection. Her plumed hat of papier-mâché is molded on her head. This is rather a rare type. In fact, Mrs. Emma C. Clear of Redondo Beach, California, says she has seen only one other like it and that was in the former Gellert collection in Oregon. The cloth body is undoubtedly a replacement. Milliners' Models form a fascinating collection. There are so many different types and sizes, and their charm is undeniable.

Papier-mâché was used for other types of dolls, and sometimes definite dates are known. A pageboy doll with kid body and papier-mâché head was found in an old trunk in an antique shop in Woodstock, Vermont. The doll was the property of Lucretia Goddard, daughter of Mehitible

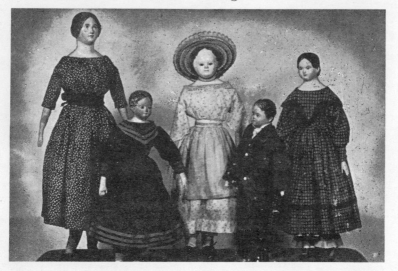

8. *Early Papier-mâché Dolls. Collection of Claire Ellegood Smith, Peterborough, N. H.*

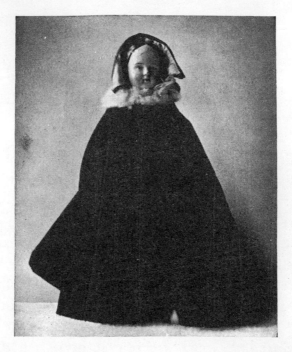

9. Large Papier-mâché Doll. Canfield Dolls of Arlington, Vt. Courtesy of Dorothy Canfield Fisher.

Dawes Goddard, who was the daughter of William Dawes, the rider with Paul Revere on the memorable night of April 18, 1775. The doll was labeled "Lucretia's doll, given her in 1028 by William Goddard, of the firm of Pratt and Goddard on Pearl St. Boston." Samuel Goddard was a cousin of Lucretia's and records show that the firm was in the importing business.

III. PRE-GREINER AND GREINER DOLLS

Germany made papier-mâché doll heads of various sizes during the early years of the nineteenth century. Most of these had glass eyes. Some dolls were almost life-sized. The larger ones with glass eyes are now called Pre-Greiner because collectors formerly thought that all papier-mâché dolls were made by Ludwig Greiner of Philadelphia. He was a German dollmaker who took out the first American patent for dolls in 1858. The Pre-Greiner dolls, made from 1840 to 1845 had, for the most part, eyes of *blown* glass, and we now know that Greiner used *painted* eyes in his dolls. Come to think of it, we have never seen a Greiner doll with blown-glass eyes and blonde hair. Have you?

Greiner made heads only; bodies were made at home. The heads were of several sizes and of different types, both blondes and brunettes. As we have said, Greiner's first patent was granted in 1858, and the labels on the shoulders of the heads bear that date. The patent was extended in 1872 and the later heads bear labels of that date.

10. Dollie and her Dollie. *Pre-Greiner papier-mâché dolls with blown-glass eyes, about 1845. Collection of Mrs. Ralph E. Wakeman, Claremont, N. H.*

11. Pre-Greiner Dolls. Collection of Katherine Frye, Andover, Mass.

12. Early Papier-mâché Dolls. Collection of Claire Ellegood Smith, Peterborough, N. H.

17

13. Original Greiner Dolls. Collection of Claire Ellegood Smith, Peterborough, N. H.

However, Greiner seems to have been at work before the date of his first patent, for we know of three heads, unquestionably Greiner, that are marked "Patent Applied For." He may also have made heads after 1872. A doll that came from Burlington, Vermont, bears evidence of wearing the Greiner label on the left side; on the right is a white label which reads, "Without linen."

Greiner's method as set forth in his patent included the use of cloth as reinforcement. Noses and chins were the weak points and when these became worn, the cloth showed through. Even without labels, the papier-mâché Greiner heads are characteristic and easily distinguished from other types. They are favorites with collectors, and since the Greiner is the first American-made doll, one or more examples should be in every general collection.

IV. M. & S. SUPERIOR DOLLS

Another type of papier-mâché doll, large and small, blonde and brunette, which is still fairly plentiful, at least in New England, is the M. & S. Superior doll. This usually has a label on the left shoulder: "M. & S. Superior No. 2015," although the wording varies as well as the number. The doll is pretty, with painted eyes and short sausage curls around the head. The hair, like that of other papier-mâché types, is molded on the head and painted. Who made this doll and where are still unsolved questions.

Some collectors believe that the M. & S. Superior heads were a product of the Greiner factories. The argument against this theory is that, while the finish on their faces is fine and beautiful when they are found in pristine condition, it is badly marred in dolls that have been played with. The Greiners, on the other hand, have come through years of hard service with their placid faces in excellent condition, except for slight damage to the ends of noses and chins.

Surely it would not have been profitable for Ludwig Greiner to have made in such evidently large quantities as the Superior, a doll that would not stand up so well as those with the already famous Greiner heads.

No, it seems clear that the M. & S. Superior doll was made abroad, but perhaps we may never know. Indeed it is one of the interesting features of doll collecting that we do *not* know all the answers. We are always speculating, always discovering new facts.

The M. & S. Superior is the only papier-mâché doll, except the Milliners'-Model, that usually had a characteristic type of commercial body. The Superior bodies were always alike—cloth stuffed with hair. Striped stockings and buttoned leather shoes, made on the feet, were a part of the doll and there was always a broad sitting base on the body. One occasionally finds a Superior head on a small homemade body, indicating that heads were sometimes sold separately. The M. & S. Superior doll is another type of which each general collection should have at least one.

V. CHINA-HEAD DOLLS

Germany has always been a land of toy-making. Deposits of clay from which to make china dolls are plentiful in Germany and, in view of the number and variety and type of workmanship of the china heads, it seems likely that they were produced in backyard kilns by individual makers. China heads are molded of clay, fired, then dipped in a glaze, and refired.

The author's collection includes two, two-and-one-half-inch china heads. One of these has long curls like an 1840 Milliners' Model. The other wears bands of hair looped under the exposed ears supposedly representing Queen Victoria in 1837.

Collectors used to think that china heads were made in England. They were called Staffordshire and Chelsea, but there is no more evidence to support the theory that English potteries made doll heads, than there is that heads were made in Bennington, Vermont. All information is to the contrary.

14. China Head, about 1850. Courtesy W. B. Mollard, Westfield, N. Y.

About the earliest type of china head is the "Biedermeier" which was intended to have a wig of soft child-hair or mohair. It is smooth without a molded headdress, and has a black tonsurelike spot about the size of a half dollar at the top, to which the wig was fastened. This doll, which dates to the Biedermeier period, 1820 to 1830, is first pictured in Max von Boehn's *Dolls and Puppets*. Most German china dolls

15. China Doll. Eighteen inches high with long ropelike curls. Collection of Mrs. George De Sylva, Los Angeles, Calif.

16. Old China Dolls. Collection of Claire Ellegood Smith, Peterborough, N. H.

have black hair and blue eyes, though some have blonde hair, and a few of the black-haired dolls have brown eyes. The brown-eyed china doll is rather rare and much sought after by collectors.

One distinguishing mark of the old china-head doll is a red line directly above the eye, to simu late an eyelid. Modern dolls do not seem to have this. Very old china dolls of the Empire period generally have the heelless shoe of that time, if their china legs have not been replaced.

*17. Blonde China Doll. Collection of Mrs. Earle
E. Andrews, Winchester, Mass.*

18. China-Head Doll, 1846, Victoria. *Collection of Catherine Richards Howard, Hope, Ark.*

Another mark of the old china doll is the very deep shoulders, much deeper than those of modern dolls. China-head dolls, as well as those of wax or papier-mâché—in fact, any shoulder dolls —are measured by the height of the head from the bottom of the bust to the top of the head. In the faces of some old china heads you will often find small black spots that resemble the beauty spots worn at court in ages past. They are not beauty spots, however, but impurities in the clay from which the heads were made.

Many china heads, especially those with unusual hair styles, are called "portrait dolls" and are named for those they are supposed to resemble—Queen Victoria, Mary Todd Lincoln, Dolly Madison, Countess Dagmar, Jenny Lind, Adelina Patti, and Alice in Wonderland. It is unlikely that these ever were actual portraits. Doubtless some fancied resemblance has caused collectors to so name them.

Jenny Lind is the possible exception. When P. T. Barnum brought Jenny Lind to America for a concert tour in 1850, the "Swedish Nightingale," took the country by storm. Whether through Barnum's clever showmanship or by popular acclaim, and we suspect it was the former, the Jenny Lind craze swept the country. Everything eatable or wearable, even articles of furniture were renamed Jenny Lind. There were

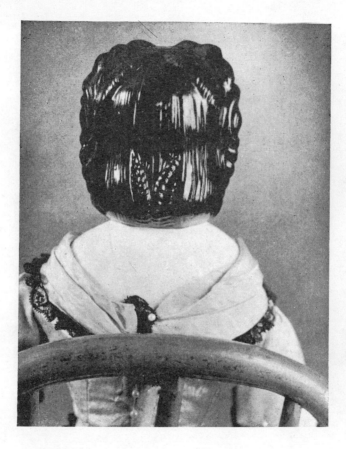

19. *China Head, rear view. Doll known as* Adelina Patti. *Collection of Mrs. George de Sylva, Los Angeles, Calif.*

20. China Doll, Jenny Lind. *Collection of Ruth Price, La Mesa, Calif.*

Jenny Lind lamps, Jenny Lind beds, and Jenny Lind neckties. At this time a number of so-called portrait dolls of Jenny Lind came over to this country. They were much alike, most of them with hair in puffs on each side of the head and drawn back to a knot, just the way the real Jenny wore her hair. (Only one type did not have the knot.) But all the dolls had black hair and Jenny was a blonde. It is said, however, that she longed for dark hair and often wore a black wig on the stage.

When Mrs. Clear produced what was the first American-made *china* doll, she chose an old model of Jenny Lind as the subject. She produced it in white and in rose-luster china. (I do not think the old Jenny Linds were ever made in the pink-tinted china.) The model proved to be most successful.

When Lewis Carroll's *Alice in Wonderland* became a best seller, little-girl dolls, representing the heroine, were made with hair slicked back to a band or circular comb of blue or black. The heads were of china, wax, Parian, or Blonde-bisque.

The *Countess Dagmar* doll in china is a replica of the familiar head in Parian that is supposed to represent the sister of the then Princess of Wales, later Queen Alexandra of England. This doll comes in many sizes and is rather more rare than the Parian head.

21. Jenny Lind. *First American-made china doll, by Emma C. Clear, Redondo Beach, Calif.*

The *Dolly Madison* head always has a round, chubby face and a cheerful expression, and there is always a black or blue ribbon drawn through her hair to a bow on top. In the china doll, it is usually black. Mrs. Clear has also made this model in a modern American china doll with a blue ribbon.

Two types of china-head dolls are called Mary Todd Lincoln, one is an apple-cheeked lady with a short, Civil War type of headdress; the other wears her hair in the chignon or waterfall popular in the 1860s. Dolls with chignons are the rarer of the two.

China heads were occasionally made with blown-glass eyes; one, at least, had sleeping eyes (that opened and shut), and a very few have swivel necks. Some, not many, have colored flowers and feathers in their hair. These dolls with fancy hair arrangements and unusual eyes are rare and therefore collectors' prizes. You are lucky if you find them, and they have considerable value.

China-head dolls were popular during most of the nineteenth century, especially after 1850. Consequently there are still a good many to collect and china heads are a happy hunting ground for present-day collectors. Another type much sought after is the "curly top" or Godey head with the hair in vertical pointed curls going straight back from the forehead and around the back. Sometimes the hair is so arranged in front, the curls running back to a black band and the hair flying loose on the neck. Mrs. Alma Hockaday owns such a head as this. The writer has the regular blonde Godey type in three-inch and six-inch sizes. Godey heads also come brunette.

22. *China-Head Doll. Exquisite old pink luster. Collection of Claire Ellegood Smith, Peterborough, N. H.*

23. *China-Head Doll. So-called "name" head, marked Ethel. St. George Collection.*

Then there is a type of black-haired china doll-head of the nineties that has straight bangs.

Early in the 1900s there appeared china heads with "jewel" necklaces of bits of colored glass embedded in a glaze. Some boy-heads were also made. From 1898, when a law was passed requiring foreign goods to indicate the country of origin, "name" heads marked "Germany" are to be found. These dolls, labeled in gold with girl's names like Helen or Ethel have collars molded

in the china. The commoner types, those with short hair similar to dolls seen in ten-cent stores today, are still imported to this country—they were never made here—but are not now so popular with children as they were in the last half of the previous century.

Occasionally glazed heads are found that were apparently made in the potteries of Dresden, Germany, from which much fine china has come. These are usually marked on the back of the shoulder with an emblem of crossed swords in blue under the glaze. They are not to be confused with the *unglazed* Parian heads.

Usually china heads were closed at the top, but German heads imported into France are found with the back of the head cut out in the same way modern German-bisque play-dolls are cut. This was done because of the French law assessing custom duties by weight. The head was lightened by cutting out sections covered by the wig. Such china heads were sometimes glazed inside as well as out.

Negro china dolls were occasionally made, particularly small penny ones. Sometimes these have colorful draperies and are supposed to be Moors, but usually they are just little Negroes, looking for all the world like the licorice candybabies of our childhood.

Color is little used in the china heads beyond blonde or black hair, blue or brown eyes, and rosy cheeks, but the writer knows two small china blonde heads with chignons, one covered with a black net, the other with green, and both wearing lettuce-green ribbons across the front of the head.

VI. WAX AND COMPOSITION DOLLS

Next to china-head dolls, the most popular type during the last half of the nineteenth century was the doll with a head of thick or of thin wax over a papier-mâché reinforcement.

Wax dolls were made in England, Germany, and France, and much earlier than the nineteenth century. How early, we do not know, but certainly the age of Queen Anne had its wax workers and wax dolls. In the nineteenth century, there were egg-shaped heads with the hair inserted in a slit down the middle, parted and drawn to each side. These dolls apparently came in about 1820. Their glass eyes were dark and without pupils and, as a rule, their leather hands had only three fingers.

About 1825 came the wire-eyed wax type, the first of the dolls with sleeping-eyes. The eyes were dark, had no pupils, and were manipulated by a wire. This came out at the side of the waist.

From 1840 to 1845 came the "Pumpkin-Head" or "Squash-Head" dolls with hair arranged in a pompadour and molded on the head. Usually there was a black band like a circular comb

24. Old Wax Doll. Collection of Ann Nichols, Claymont, Del.

around the top of the head and the dark glass eyes also had no pupils. Arms and legs were of wood. The bodies were usually stuffed with straw or hay.

Mme. Augusta Montanari's thick wax models first attracted attention at the Crystal Palace Exposition in London in 1851, when she exhibited dolls of both sexes and all ages. They were a sensation at the show and probably the first character dolls ever shown. All were appropriately dressed for the age and person represented, and there were also child dolls. It is said these were the first ever made. Before this time, dolls were always made as adults with slender waists.

Little is known of Mme. Montanari except what has been gleaned from advertisements in the business sections of the London Post Office Directory. Unfortunately, some of those are missing from the Library of Congress in Washington, so we do not know even the year of her death. Her husband, Napoleon, was apparently a sculptor in wax. Her son worked with her in the making of wax dolls. He seems also to have made rag dolls, although none have ever been identified. The son continued in the business at least until 1887 and perhaps till the 1890s. Here again the absence of some volumes in the Directory leaves in doubt the exact year he ceased operations in London.

The Montanari dolls—as might be expected

25. Wax Dolls, 1880. Collection of Mrs. John Alexander, South Royalton, Vt.

from the studio of a wax sculptor—are among the most artistic ever modeled. They are the thick-wax type and without the reinforcement of papier-mâché or other material. The eyes are of glass, deep violet-blue in the earlier dolls, a lighter blue threaded grey in the later ones, which were very likely imported from Germany.

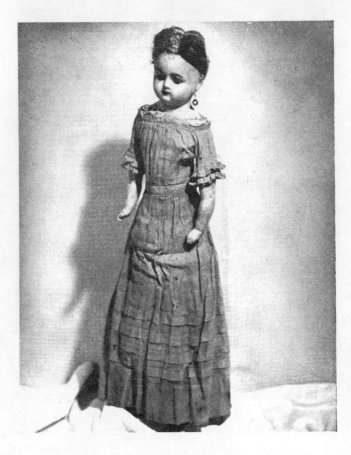

26. Old Wax Doll. Collection of Warren County Historical Museum, Lebanon, O.

27. *Wax Dolls. Probably Mexican. Collection of Marion Smith, Burlington, Vt.*

In the earlier violet-blue eyes, Mrs. Clear thinks she has discovered traces of the same blue used in decorating Staffordshire pottery, and so it is supposed that these eyes were made in England. By 1849 nearly all dolls everywhere were being made with blue eyes, in compliment to the young blue-eyed Queen Victoria who had come to the throne in 1837 and was a leading figure in world politics.

There are no wigs on the Montanari dolls; each hair is set directly into the wax with a hot needle and looks the way human hair does on the scalp. Sometimes eyebrows and eyelashes are similarly set in. Hands are feet are usually of wax.

In 1855 the Montanaris exhibited in the Paris Exposition where their work was favorably received. Whether in imitation of the Montanari, or as original work, the French afterwards made thick-wax dolls with set-in hair and wax hands and feet. As an example of the French use of the Montanari method, Mr. and Mrs. Grant Holt of Keene, New Hampshire, brought from Paris a beautiful thick-wax Christ Child, which is most lovely.

From 1855 until the 1890s, wax dolls equaled china-head dolls in popularity in England and America, but in the late 1890s they were superseded by German-bisque dolls. Perhaps wax dolls lost favor because they were so perishable. Bisque dolls stood a good deal more wear and tear without showing it.

From Germany about 1870 to 1880 came a flood of cheaper wax dolls: wax over papier-mâché with mohair wigs. Often the pompadours and rolls were molded in the head itself and sometimes there were pierced ears with earrings. Bodies were stuffed with straw and usually there was an oblong voice or noise box, which emitted

28. Hilda. *Quaint doll of wax over papier-mâché. Blown-glass eyes. Collection of Claire Ellegood Smith, Peterborough, N. H.*

a squeak when pressed. As a rule, feet and hands were composition, but some were of carved wood —possibly it would be more correct to say of "turned wood" as they were obviously machine-made. Occasionally one finds wooden arms from the elbow down and wooden hands on wax dolls that have composition feet. Generally these old wax dolls, especially cheaper ones, are in rather poor condition when found, but they are easily rewaxed and restored and are worth doing. (For firms specializing in this work see page 160.)

In the early days of collecting, the wax doll was neglected in favor of other types, with the result that now wax dolls are relatively more plentiful and less expensive than most of the others. They therefore offer an excellent field to present-day collectors. Indeed it seems that earlier collectors have missed a real opportunity in more or less neglecting this type, except for the Montanari dolls, which have always been prized. A clever person, starting today with the egg-shaped heads of the 1820 period—those having the hair set in slits in the heads—and continuing through the wire-eyed waxes down to the wax dolls of the 1890s, can assemble a collection of beauty and rarity at a fairly reasonable cost.

There is one wax doll that has not been mentioned—the type wearing a molded "walking" hat with three plumes—sometimes called the

Empress Eugenie of France, although it is doubtful if it was ever intended to represent that "glass of fashion." Mrs. Cyrus M. Beachy, a well-known collector of Wichita, Kansas, who is well past eighty years old, says she recalls wearing an identical hat when she was a child. So the walking hat probably commemorates youthful, rather than imperial, apparel.

Wax dolls seem to have been among the first to display teeth. Up to 1880 most dolls had closed lips, but Marion Smith of Burlington, Vermont, has a wax doll with two teeth and Mrs. Erwin Chapin of Silver Creek, New York, has one with two teeth that are wooden pegs.

About 1870, and probably in Germany, a number of smooth composition dolls were made of wood flour, starch, and rosin mixed with water. They had mohair wigs, closed lips, often deep violet-blue glass eyes, and in most cases composition hands and feet. They were very pretty and apparently not expensive.

In France a composition doll was made with painted hair. Usually it was finer than the German ones and beautifully dressed. Today these composition types are more appreciated in France, American collectors do not know them well.

VII. PARIAN OR DRESDEN DOLLS

Doll-making entered a new and fascinating stage with the "bisque" heads. Bisque heads are *unglazed*. China heads are also made from clay, but are subsequently dipped in a glaze and fired.

Today the most sought-after dolls, and therefore the most expensive, ranging from one hundred to five hundred dollars each, are those with unglazed Parian or Blonde-bisque Dresden heads. Why collectors think them worth so much is something of a mystery. The Parian head is white, like marble. The Blonde-bisque has delicate coloring in hair, eyes, lips, cheeks, and ornaments, but the term "Parian" through usage is now applied to both. Parian heads are made from the same type of clay as the more common glazed china heads, but Parians are left unglazed, as are the coarser type known as Stone-bisque. Early and later Parians and Stone-bisque heads differ mainly in the degree of fineness to which the clay is ground. The Parian and Blonde-bisque heads were made between 1850 and 1870,

February 1967

S	M	T	W	T	F	S
			1	2	3	4
5	6	7	8	9	10	11
12	13	14	15	16	17	18
19	20	21	22	23	24	25
26	27	28				

January

S	M	T	W	T	F	S
1	2	3	4	5	6	7
8	9	10	11	12	13	14
15	16	17	18	19	20	21
22	23	24	25	26	27	28
29	30	31				

March

S	M	T	W	T	F	S
			1	2	3	4
5	6	7	8	9	10	11
12	13	14	15	16	17	18
19	20	21	22	23	24	25
26	27	28	29	30	31	

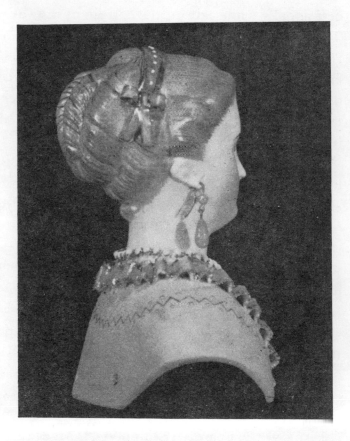

29. Caroline Channing. *Rare Parian head with luster trim. Courtesy of Mrs. Edmond Poetter, Reading, Vt.*

or perhaps a little later. The finest and smoothest are from the 1850 to 1860 decade.

Usually the Parians were elaborately decorated with colored feathers, flowers, scarves, ribbons, combs, jewels, and luster ruffs—single, double, occasionally triple—about the bottom of the yoke. The hair, blonde for the most part but occasionally brunette, was arranged in interesting and elaborate ways. The eyes were painted or of blown glass, oval with high centers—the "paperweight" type. The glass-eyed dolls are preferred by collectors.

Heads measure from two and one half to six inches high. They are beautiful both in design and workmanship, a product in which any potter might take pride, but curiously enough there is no mention—not a single word about them— in any book on the china made at the Dresden factories. Curious? Yes, but the reason is not far to seek. These beautiful heads were regarded as commercial hack work by the men who made them and unworthy to carry the name or mark of the pottery.

The Parian heads made at the Dresden factories (if we consider the internal evidence conclusive), were apparently shipped to America as holiday novelties to be sold by jewelers, confectioners, and other shopkeepers. There are at least two authenticated instances of this. Before the Civil War, the German grandfather of Miss

30. Amelia Bloomer. *Parian doll. St. George Collection.*

Amelia Robeck settled in Annapolis, Maryland, as a baker and confectioner. In her collection Miss Robeck has a doll, which she acquired from the estate of an Annapolis woman in its original wrappings, who had purchased it in her grandfather's store. The doll must have been bought about 1860 for the store was looted and destroyed by Union soldiers when Annapolis fell into their hands that year. Further proof comes from Mrs. Otis Carl Williams of Jamestown, Rhode Island, whose grandfather was a jeweler in Providence, Rhode Island. As a child, playing one day in her grandfather's barn, she found a box containing a number of Dresden doll heads—apparently unsold merchandise. Her grandfather gave them to her, but her mother, an early collector, confiscated them, gave them bodies, and dressed them. Today, Mrs. Williams and her sister, who divided their mother's collection, each have several wonderful Parian or Dresden dolls.

These two instances illustrate the purpose for which these Parian heads were made; their apparent low cost at that time indicate they were not highly regarded either by maker or purchaser. Today they are dressed by collectors in elaborate costumes of silk, satin and lace, and are considered among their choicest items.

As we have indicated, the best of the Parian or Dresden dolls were made between 1850 and 1860. Most of the heads after 1860 were of coarser

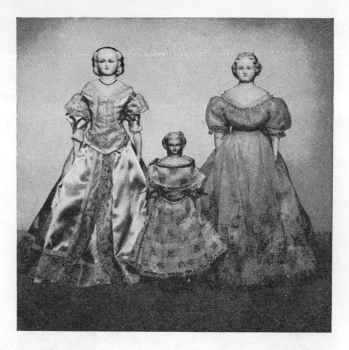

31. Parian Dolls. Collection of Mrs. Leo Lamb, Santa Ana, Calif.

clay and not so fine in modeling. Of course there are exceptions, and indeed there is great variation even in heads of the same model. We have seen *Countess Dagmar* heads that were fine and lovely and others that were really hack work.

One of the most beautiful heads made before 1860 and a favorite among collectors, if we are to judge by the number who have it, is the *Empress Eugenie,* which may have been intended for a portrait of the young Empress of France. This doll is found in many parts of the country.

32. Parian Doll. Rose in hair. Collection of Katherine Anderson, Worcester, Mass.

Mrs. Edmund Porter of Reading, Vermont, for instance, has three—two of different sizes in the same design, the other slightly different. On each the golden hair is arranged in a chignon or waterfall with a green or black net. On one side of the front of the head is an elaborate decoration of pinkish gold luster; on the other side there is some silver luster. Some collectors mistakenly call this hair net a "snood" but the "silken snood" is something quite different—a ribbon which the Scotch maiden bound in her hair as a token of her virginity.

The *Toinette* or *Mary Antoinette* doll is supposed to represent another Empress of France as she played at farming in the Petite Trianon with her maids. This doll wears roses in her hair. Another favorite is the *Catherine Channing* head which has the luster ruff and an elaborate arrangement of hair with jeweled combs. The *Countess Dagmar,* popular in both Parian and china, came out about 1870.

Collectors often include among their dolls fine modern reproductions as well as original old ones. Replicas of many types have been made with great skill and artistry. In California, Mrs. Clear has produced beside the *Jenny Lind,* outstanding china-head types and some good Parians. One of her latest Blonde-bisques is a replica of the *Toinette* doll, very lovely and delicately colored, with three hand-carved pink roses in the

33. Bonnet Dolls. Collection of Mrs. Byron M. Peckham, Yorkshire, N. Y.

56

blonde hair. Mrs. Clear has also made some originals. Those representing George and Martha Washington equal the best of the old Dresdens; in some ways, they are even finer and are included in many discriminating collections. Mrs. Clear's dolls were designed by the distinguished American artist, Martha Oathout Ayres.

The "Bonnet" dolls, so-called because their hats or bonnets of various types are molded on their heads, are made of Stone-bisque and are small and medium-sized. These are favorites with some collectors among them Mrs. Byron Peckham, part of whose collection is shown here. Mrs. Peckham also collects papier-mâchés, Dresdens, china-heads, and others.

VIII. JUMEAU DOLLS

Germany has always been the land of doll-makers and for generations France has imported bisque and china heads from there. About 1862, M. Jumeau, the leading French dollmaker, decided to end this dependence on Germany by creating a bisque head that would be French in every particular. For this purpose he employed artists to design a head of great beauty in Blonde-bisque. It was to be superior in every way, and so it turned out. The eyes were a lovely feature, deep and luminous, made of blown glass. There is no mistaking the eyes of a Jumeau doll for anything else. Some fanciful collectors have called them "spun glass eyes," but actually there is no such thing as a *spun glass* eye. Wigs were tacked to a cork fitted into a large opening in the head. At first they were made of the hair of the Tibetan goat, later of mohair.

M. Jumeau's fame as a dollmaker dates from 1844. He was then using German heads but dressing his dolls in handsome clothes. A commentator on the Crystal Palace Exposition in London

34. Jumeau Dolls, after 1880. Collection of Mr. and Mrs. Grant Holt, Keene, N. H.

in 1851, where M. Jumeau exhibited, remarks on the beautiful clothes but calls the dolls quite ordinary. When the Jumeau French-bisque heads came out, they were considered superior to all others.

At first head and shoulders were in one piece, but about 1869 Jumeau's eldest son invented a swivel neck, which was a decided improvement. Bodies on Jumeau dolls went through a long evolution. They were made in fourteen sizes. The earliest were jointed kid stuffed with sawdust, but when handled the joints on these also

35. Jumeau French-Fashion Doll. Dress said to have been copied from the gown made for Empress Eugenie of France. Collection of Mrs. E. H. Poetter, Reading, Vt.

filled with sawdust and the dolls would not stand up. So a jointed wooden body was made with the kid drawn over it like a suit of long underwear; then there was a wooden and kid body, each joint and member having the kid shrunken on before assembling, and in progression, a stockinet, a cloth, and an all-wood body. A cotton

36. *French-Fashion Dolls. Collection of Claire Ellegood Smith, Peterborough, N. H.*

body with leather arms was made for the cheaper Jumeau dolls, but until 1880 the bisque shoulder-head was used on all.

In that year, M. Jumeau's son invented a composition body—similar to that of modern dolls—but first made in the Jumeau factory. It was strung together with elastic cord and the shoulder was abandoned in favor of a head sunk into the body, as in the modern types. Until these dolls appeared, the Jumeaus were seldom marked except in unusual cases.

Besides these body variations there were transitional hands and feet. The material of these evidently depended on what was at hand. The fact seems to be that the Jumeaus used leftovers from one body to finish the next until all was used up. The one constant factor is the beauty of the eyes.

IX. FRENCH-FASHION DOLLS

There was one street in Paris, around le passage du Choiseul that was almost entirely occupied by the makers of doll costumes, doll wigs, and accessories. Like the earlier Milliners' Models of papier-mâché, these later French types were really fashion dolls. Everything that a fashionable lady could and should wear was reproduced for these dolls—underwear, corsets, dresses, fancy shoes, kid gloves, jewels, combs, fans, and parasols. These all appeared in a doll's apparel. A trousseau might consist of three to sixteen costumes for as many different occasions and each complete with jewels and accessories.

Another French dollmaker of importance was M. Bru, who made a different type of bisque doll, with heavier features and darker coloring than the Jumeau. At first Bru dolls had kid bodies. Later they were wooden and jointed, similar to some used for a time by Jumeau. (Indeed it appears that this jointed wooden body was actually invented by Bru.) One of the most beautiful kid bodies that we have ever seen was on a Bru doll.

37–38. Bru Twins. Collection of Nellie McLachlan and Marian

*Howard, formerly The Doll House,
Miami, Fla.*

39. French-Fashion Dolls. Collection of Anna Doyle, Jamaica Plains, Mass.

40. French-Fashion Dolls (back view of Plate 39).

Bru used the shoulder-head with the swivel neck and he usually set an incised mark on the left shoulder:
B
R
U

French-bisque dolls have also come from smaller houses. Sometimes the dolls were actually made in Germany; sometimes they were made in France from parts imported from Germany, as was the case with the "Bébé Steiner." This has always been known as a French doll, but we have it on the authority of a leading French dollmaker today that it was only assembled in France.

Undoubtedly the French-bisque head, as made by Jumeau, represents the best in dollmaking and it is understandable that this doll is the most sought for by collectors, with the exception of the Dresden. The price of the Jumeaus is constantly increasing and they are a good buy, especially when found with original costumes intact. Today most of them found are not likely to be discovered with more than one costume and the accessories are usually pretty well dispersed.

Both Jumeau and Bru made a few brown bisque dolls to represent Negroes, but these are seldom seen in collections and are very scarce. The Germans also made brown bisque dolls for the South Pacific. These dolls for peoples of mixed races often come with blue eyes.

41. French-Fashion Doll. Collection of Mrs. Henry S. Diament, N. Y.

42. French-Fashion Doll. Collection of Elizabeth MacMahon, Everett, Mass.

43. Old Negro Dolls, Collection of Claire Elle-good Smith, Peterborough, N. H.

In the writer's collection is a mammy doll with black bisque head and black cloth body. The head has no wig and the bald surface is covered by a knotted bandana turban. Nothing is known of its origin but it is undoubtedly a German-bisque head, since all bisques were German except the Jumeaus.

Most of the old Negro dolls are composition; a few are of wood, and once in a while one sees a head in wax. Mrs. Elsie Clark Krug, Krug's International Doll House in Baltimore, recently imported a peddler doll from England that had a black wax face with the features of a crone or witch, rather than of a Negro. It was one of the old peddler dolls from about 1780. The body is wood with the legs inserted in a wooden base.

The two Negro dolls shown here are from the collection of Mrs. Alexander Smith of Peterborough, New Hampshire. Mrs. Smith has one of the choicest doll collections in the country, numbering about two thousand items. She includes modern foreign-costume dolls as well as antique dolls.

X. GERMAN-BISQUE DOLLS

Germany has turned out the largest number of bisque dolls of any country, as well as wooden, wax, china, Dresden, and other sorts. Nuremberg and Sonnenburg were the centers of the toymaking industry for centuries, but in World War II, Nuremberg was bombed out and travelers report that not a single dollmaker or doll kiln remained.

There is a mine of information on German-bisque dolls, untapped by collectors, in German books listed in the bibliography of the American edition of Max von Boehn's excellent book, *Dolls and Puppets,* now out of print. There are numerous marks and figures on the shoulders and the backs of the heads of the German-bisques of which we do not know the meaning. Here is a whole field to be investigated and a wonderful opportunity for the doll collector who knows German.

Since 1880 practically all German-bisques have had open lips and teeth. Previously lips were

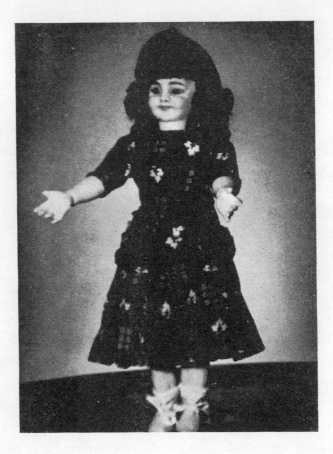

44. German-Bisque Two-Face Doll. Rare. Collection of Mrs. Arthur Hilsdorf, Syracuse, N. Y.

45. German-Bisque Two-Face Doll. Unusual with one negro face, Collection of Mrs. Arthur Hilsdorf, Syracuse, N. Y.

46. German-Bisque, Blue-Scarf Doll. Collection of Anna Doyle, Jamaica Plains, Mass.

47. German-Bisque Doll, about 1880. St. George Collection.

usually closed. The cheaper dolls have stationary eyes; the more expensive have sleeping eyes that open and close by counterweights.

One of the finest of German dolls is the Royal Kaestner which is about fifty or more years old. It has a fine jointed kid body on which is stamped the mark of a crown encircled with a ribbon ending in a bowknot. The Royal Kaestners have beautiful faces and lovely eyes. They usually come in large sizes and are favorites of collectors.

The dolls of Armand Marseilles are also about fifty years old and more plentiful than the Royal Kaestners. They are less expensive but popular too. They have a cheaper kid body and on the back of the necks "A.M.," is incised with certain numerals.

Some fine German-bisque dolls are labeled Heinrich Handwerck. We are not sure whether this is the mark of the manufacturer or of the actual maker of the dolls. In any case the Handwerck dolls are among the finest. The name is often combined with others, as S & H, which stands for Simon & Halbig.

K. and R. dolls (Kammerer and Reinhart), were made in various sizes before the turn of the century and are very beautiful. They are marked with the Jewish six-pointed Star of David and have the letters K and R in the points. From the stock of an old store in the Middle West, the

48. German-Bisque Doll. Molded Hair. Courtesy of Mrs. Ralph E. Wakeman, Claremont, N. H.

writer bought several heads which were ink stamped with the familiar star mark in an oval and the word "Germany" below. These heads were evidently made before 1891 when Congress passed a law requiring imported merchandise to carry the name of the country of origin; later

49. German-Bisque Doll. Collection of Mrs. Ralph E. Wakeman, Claremont, N. H.

K. and R. dolls have the mark incised. All bisque dolls made after 1891 have "Germany" incised as well as the other marks.

Another German doll, marked with an incised horseshoe and the name Floradora, apparently originated about the time of the famous Sextette —1898 through 1903.

XI. CHARACTER AND FLIRTING-EYE DOLLS

For the most part, character dolls represent certain well-known persons—Shirley Temple, Sonja Henie, to mention two. They include dolls that looked like real babies. Usually they were of composition or bisque. "Character" dolls are not to be confused with "name" dolls which were made in Germany, and had girls' names labeled in gold in the china.

German bisque dolls are usually of the baby-face type. The first of these was the homely new-born infant type with composition body. Collectors sometimes call this the Kaiser Wilhelm or the German Crown Prince doll. Since the accession of Queen Juliana, it has become the Crown Princess Juliana. Actually it was modeled from the three-day-old son of the workman who made it. It comes in various sizes—up to thirty-two inches.

Many American-designed dolls like Grace Story Putnam's well-known Bye-lo Baby were

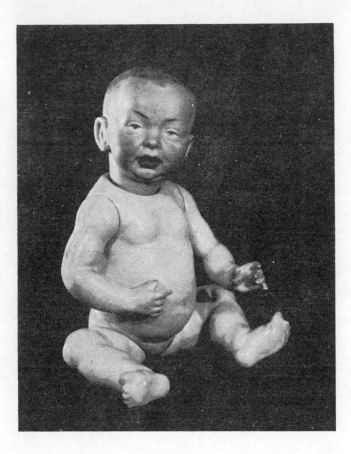

50. German-Bisque Doll. First of the character dolls. St. George Collection.

cast in Germany. It would be hard to say how many of the various sizes of this charming infant head were turned out from her wax model, but for some time the yearly royalties amounted to seventy thousand dollars. The Bye-lo Baby revolutionized the doll market and resulted in a flood of infant and character dolls both in bisque and composition. Georgine Averill of Hollywood also had her models for baby dolls cast in Germany.

For some years, Rose O'Neill's perky little Kewpie dolls delighted the world. They came in various sizes in bisque and in composition. The bisques were made in Germany, and probably the others were too. Playhouse dolls, representing all ages and conditions, have been made in Germany for at least fifty years. The author has two. One is an officer and one a gentleman in evening dress; both were brought from Germany in 1908. Two world wars have interrupted German toy production and dollmaking for considerable periods, but the industries always come back.

Among the character dolls, both bisque and composition, that followed Bye-lo Baby in the last twenty years and are now sought by collectors are the Patsy doll and dolls representing Shirley Temple, Jane Withers, Sonja Henie, and the Dionne quintuplets in various stages of development—to mention a few.

51. Sonja Henie. *Composition character doll.*
Collection of Allie Vigneau, San Diego, Calif.

Assembling a collection of German-bisques is
easy because the supply is good and the dolls
relatively inexpensive. They are beautiful too
and lend themselves to a variety of costumes, an
invitation to the imaginative to dress them. Indeed they make a handsome display.

Outstanding collections of this type belong to
Mrs. Aline Vigneau of California and to Mrs.
Mae Connors of Dorchester, Massachusetts. The
general collection of Mrs. Rose Parro of Water-
bury, Vermont, includes many interesting Ger-

52. Shirley Temple. *Composition doll. Collection of Allie Vigneau, San Diego, Calif.*

man-bisques. She has sixteen hundred dolls in all.

The eyes of the bisques are of blown glass, with pupils, and beautifully colored irises which are finely threaded. These are made in Germany, which has long specialized in optical glass and artificial eyes, an industry which has been supplemented by the making of similar eyes for dolls.

The "flirting-eye" doll in bisque or composition has been made in Germany for a hundred years at least. It is so called because eyes move from side to side instead of up and down. Ear-

53. Snow White and the Seven Dwarfs. *Made in England. Collectio* *of Mrs. Otto Wolff, Lincoln, Mass.*

lier ones were composition. Mrs. Edmund H. Poetter of Reading, Vermont, has one of these in her collection and a similar doll in bisque was brought from Germany in 1908 to the writer's sister, Mrs. Robert H. Carey of Front Royal, Virginia.

Many small novelty dolls were also made in bisque in German factories where true artists were employed at the low wages of unskilled workmen. With cheap labor, Germany could undersell the United States in open markets and so hold a monopoly in the doll and toy markets.

XII. SPRINGFIELD DOLLS

Two types of wooden dolls represent the contribution of this country to the history of old dolls. These are the Springfield dolls from Vermont, and the Schoenhut dolls made in Philadelphia.

A Vermont man, Joel Ellis, who was an inventive genius, patented thirteen different articles, among them a steam shovel, a baby carriage or cab for which he was nicknamed Cab Ellis, and the now-famous Ellis wooden doll. As a young man, Ellis bought a timber tract on the Black River near Springfield, and with his partners, established a woodworking shop for the manufacture of baby carriages, sleds, carts, and wagons. Scraps from this work were used to make the Ellis doll carriage, modeled on the baby cabs.

In 1873 Ellis took out a patent for a wooden doll of rock maple with mortise and tenon joints, and pewter or iron hands and feet. Heads were of blocks of wood taken from the end of the grain and rounded, except for one pointed side

87

54. Wooden Doll. Dressed as a Burmese married woman. Nineteenth Century. Victoria and Albert Museum, London.

55. Queen Anne Wooden Doll. Courtesy of B. H. Leffingwell, Rochester, N. Y.

which allowed for the nose. Each block was put into a steel mold and shaped under hydraulic pressure. When it came out of the press, holes were drilled to fit a large tenon that had been made on the end of the body. The head, which was stationary, was glued to the body by means of this large tenon. The doll came in twelve-, fifteen-, and eighteen-inch heights. The most plentiful is the twelve-inch, the least, the eighteen-inch.

The bodies and the eight leg and arm sections of each doll were turned on a lathe and then put together with the Ellis-patented mortise and tenon joints and steel pins. The head, lower limbs, and forearms were dipped in flesh-colored paint; the features, eyes, and hair were painted by women, notably by two cousins of Joel Ellis, the Misses Woodbury, who became painters of miniatures.

The assembling of the dolls and much of the other work on them was done by women. The feet of the Ellis models are always jointed, enabling the dolls to assume various positions; being all wood, they are not easily broken. With the passing of time it is evident that the paint on these dolls is the weakest point and few dolls today have much left on heads and faces. The metal hands and feet are often missing too and sometimes the mortise and tenon joints are broken.

56. Wooden Doll. Type loved by Queen Victoria when a child. Collection of Mrs. Cyrus Beachy, Wichita, Kans.

Ellis made both blondes and brunettes, and occasionally, on order, a few Negro dolls by the simple expedient of painting the faces black. Features were never changed, all being made in the same mold.

In the 1873 depression, Ellis dolls were not ordered in sufficient quantity to warrant manufacture after the fall season. In fact no more were ever made although Ellis manufactured other toys—a piano and stool, dining table and chairs, a small bed, rail fences, log cabins, and such.

Six or seven years later, Mason and Taylor undertook the manufacture of wooden dolls. Luke Taylor of Springfield, Vermont, was also an inventor and an excellent mechanic as well. He made the machines on which the dolls were made. The earliest type had a hemispherical joint patented by a man named Martin, a cabinetmaker of sorts. It does not appear that he was the inventor of the Martin joint but merely had it patented for someone who bought it from the inventor.

Basing the opinion on patent records, collectors for some years thought that the Martin model represented another dollmaking venture, but even cursory examination reveals that it was made on the same machines which Luke Taylor built for the Mason and Taylor doll. The Martin is the rarest of the Springfield dolls, there being, as far as we know, only five of them in existence: the author owns two; one was discovered in Lyme, New Hampshire; one in Ludlow, Vermont, and the fifth, minus head and arms in Fairlee, Vermont. Like the later Mason and Taylor models, the Martin doll is about eleven inches high, the body of soft wood, the limbs of rock maple, and the head stationary. It is the only one of the Springfield dolls, except the Joel Ellis, which has feet painted black.

The Mason and Taylor doll came out in 1880. It has a soft-wood body and hardwood limbs like the so-called Martin doll, but the joints are of

57. *Wooden Dolls. Springfield, Vt.*

different design. The feet are painted bright blue.

These Mason and Taylor dolls vary with the period of manufacture. Earlier dolls have stationary heads, wooden "spoon" hands, and metal feet. Later metal hands were made, but it is to be noted that hands and fingers are in a different position from those on the Ellis doll. After 1882 the Johnson head was used. It turns on a swivel neck and looks different from the stationary head.

Occasionally experimental dolls were turned

93

out by the Mason and Taylor factory; for example, an infant doll with bald head and composition hands; and recently we heard of another that has wooden feet. A few Negro dolls were made on order, but like those by Joel Ellis, they were the standard doll painted black. In the manual of the Doll Collectors of America, one of these painted models is shown with the statement that it is an East Indian doll, but Mr. Henry Taylor, the son of Luke and himself a worker on the dolls, maintains that no Hindu dolls were made and only few of the standard dolls were painted black to look like Negroes. "To have made negroid features," said Mr. Taylor, "would have necessitated new molds, and molds are expensive."

It has been our pleasure to have known Mr. Taylor and to have discussed the dolls with him, so we have first-hand information on them. We also have had direct information on the Ellis dolls from the late Herbert Ellis, a son of Joel, with whom we had extensive correspondence.

The Mason and Taylor factory made various other articles of wood and turned out dolls only for a short period at holiday time. Their novel "Witch and Wizard" doll evidently was made for export to Japan. It was accompanied by a knife (apparently none remain today) with which to cut off the head, but the swivel neck was so arranged that the doll did not lose its head despite attempted decapitation. The limbs lack elbow and knee joints and the metal feet are in the form of oriental slippers with turned-up toes. The slippers, like the feet of other Mason and Taylor dolls except the Martin, were painted Dutch blue. The doll has oriental features and wears a gay kimono. This oriental doll was not original with Mason and Taylor. A contemporary account of the Crystal Palace Exposition at London in 1851 mentions a similar model exhibited by a German dollmaker.

XIII. SCHOENHUT DOLLS

The Schoenhut wooden dolls made in Philadelphia from 1911 to 1924 are, like the Springfield dolls, an American contribution, although
the maker was a German emigrant, the descend-
ant of German wood carvers and toymakers. The
Schoenhut is also distinguished by an unusual
joint, not of wood but of metal, and so strong
as to be virtually unbreakable and so pliable as
to let the doll assume any position. A small
metal stand made to fit into a hole in the foot
enabled the doll to stand alone while assuming
unusual positions. Mrs. Clear considers the
Schoenhut wooden doll "the finest play doll ever
brought out."

The first Schoenhuts were sixteen inches tall
and had either carved wooden "hair" or wigs.
They were charmingly dressed as boys or girls.
Later, other sizes were made. The method was
similar to that of the early Ellis doll, bodies being turned out on a lathe, heads shaped and
then molded under pressure and heat. Finally
the whole doll was given several coats of oil

58. *Schoenhut Girl Dolls. Carved hair. Eighteen inches tall. Collection of Lydia Bowerman, Clinton, O.*

paint, which did not come off when washed by a small owner.

About 1915 the Schoenhut firm brought out an attractive standard line of infant dolls from nineteen to twenty-one inches long with "Nature arms and legs," and also the "Schoenhut Manikin for Artists and Window Displays." Only about a thousand manikins were made and many

59. *Schoenhut Girl Dolls. Collection of Lydia Bower-man, Port Clinton, O.*

60. *Schoenhut Boy Dolls with carved hair. Sixteen inches tall. Collection of Lydia Bowerman, Port Clin-ton, O.*

*61. Schoenhut Boy Dolls. Collection of Lydia Bower-
man, Port Clinton, O.*

were destroyed when the company dissolved, so
these are by far the rarest of the Schoenhut dolls.
In 1919 came four models with doll faces instead
of the former character faces. The same year the
"Walkable Doll" was made in various sizes and
two years later, dolls with imitation bisque heads
and "Movable Unbreakable Wooden Eyes, Imitation Glass Eyes"—a real innovation for wooden
models—as the catalogue stated.

62. Schoenhut Wooden Dolls. Collection of Lydia Bowerman, Port Clinton, O.

The depression of the 1920s led to the cheapening of the Schoenhut dolls. Steel joints were replaced by rubber cord for stringing and later dolls had cloth not wooden bodies, but in the end the company went into bankruptcy and the business was discontinued.

Perhaps the most interesting work of the Schoenhuts was the wooden Bye-lo Baby head. Why they undertook this is hard to understand, for it was an infringement of the Putnam paten. At any rate, few were made and these are a real prize for collectors.

For centuries the Germans carved wooden dolls, and so did the English. In colonial times, homemade wooden dolls were almost the only ones the children had and these still turn up occasionally. Some are so-called "penny dolls," one or two inches tall, pegged and jointed; others are nine or ten inches tall, sometimes jointed, sometimes not. Since they were handmade in the home, wooden dolls are individual, depending on the skill and ingenuity of the maker. In themselves they make an interesting collection.

64. *Ravaca Dolls. French peasants by Bernard Ravaca. Collection of Claire Ellegood Smith, Peterborough, N. H.*

Martha Jenks Chase of Pawtucket, Rhode Island, had one of these as a child and was inspired by it to make rag dolls for her own children, then for the neighbors', and so began the famous Chase dolls. Mrs. Chase made them commercially as playthings for children and later as demonstration dolls for hospitals and nursing classes. The Chase factory is still a going concern.

*65. Fabric Dolls. Made by Mrs. Frances Ravaca,
N. Y. Collection of Claire Ellegood Smith, Peterborough, N. H.*

At the New York World's Fair at Flushing
Meadows in 1939 and 1940 the French exhibit
included the dolls of Bernard Ravaca. He was a
Parisian dollmaker already world-famous for his
fabric dolls with faces made from silk stockings.
They represented French peasants and other
character types.

World War II caught M. Ravaca over here.
His studios in Paris having been looted, he re-

66. Lenci Dolls. Collection of Elizabeth Mac-Mahon, Everett, Mass.

mained, to become an American citizen. Mme. Ravaca, the former Eleanor Deicks of Cohoes, New York, is also a doll artist. The Ravacas tour the country exhibiting their dolls in the larger cities in the United States and Canada. Their models have delighted American collectors.

In Italy, before the war, the late Mme. Lenci made a doll of felt treated with air pressure. It was both quaint and beautiful. Her dolls usually represented children, but she also made a boudoir doll of the dancer Raquel Miller which was very beautiful. Mme. Lenci was a true artist and her dolls were unique. Since her death, the factories have reopened, but the loss of the master designer is sadly felt.

Kathe Kruse's dolls in prewar Germany came into being in much the same way as Martha Chase's in New England. Frau Kruse first made dolls for her own children and then commercially. She created the most appealing and real children imaginable. During the war her dolls were banned, but happily she is again at work.

When World War I checked the flow of dolls from Germany, two California artists, Mr. and Mrs. P. D. Smith, and their young daughter Margaret undertook the making of baby dolls from a composition of their own. The dolls were well received on the West Coast, but being handmade, proved unprofitable. Later the Smiths turned out some lovely display figures for shop windows. Most of their work has now disappeared, but a few examples remain in the possession of fortunate California collectors.

XV. CARE OF OLD DOLLS

Dust, moths, and in some cases, extremes of temperature are the enemies of old dolls. A tight cupboard with glass doors offers the best safeguard from dust. Second-best protection is to cover the dolls singly or in groups with glass domes such as covered wax flowers and stuffed birds in Victorian parlors. These are no longer manufactured, but may sometimes be bought in antique shops, though the old ones are getting scarce and of course are hard to ship as they break easily.

Another useful device for protecting small dolls is a shadow box. Behind the opening of a deep oval or square Victorian picture frame you may have built a box of composition or wood some three inches deep. Line it with velvet or a small-patterned wallpaper to suit the decoration of a room and place a strip of velvet on the floor for a carpet. The dolls are then arranged in the box which can be fastened to the picture frame

67. *Rare Composition Doll. All parts original.*
Collection of Claire Ellegood Smith, Peter-
borough, N. H.

with a hook and two screw eyes on each side of the box.

Whatever the dust protection used, it is wise also to sprinkle paradichloride-benzene crystals to deter moths. In the cupboard, you can use small bags of crystals, concealed here and there under a doll's long dress. When a large doll with a wig is exposed in a room, sprinkle the crystals in the hair occasionally and when it is not on exhibit, tie cellophane over the head, fastening it tightly around the neck.

Wax dolls should be kept at room temperatures of sixty to eighty degrees, Fahrenheit, and should never be exposed to extremes of heat and cold, as in shipping. Extreme heat will melt the wax and extreme cold will cause it to crack and peel.

Papier-mâché dolls, particularly Milliners' Models with small heads, are also damaged by extreme cold and should not be shipped in winter or the finish may crack. We have seen more than one fine old Milliners' Model ruined by being exposed to very cold weather.

Wire stands of various sizes for displaying dolls are again on the market. Stands with plastic bases for small dolls may be had at some five-and-ten-cent stores. Dolls look much neater when mounted on stands.

68. Fortune-Telling Dolls. Collection of Mr. and Mrs. Grant Holt, Keene, N. H.

XVI. DOLLS FOR DRESSMAKING

The doll hobby has developed a new profes-
sion, that of doll dressmaking open to all women
who sew well. Many are now making a good liv-
ing from it, often charging as much today for a
doll outfit as formerly they charged for a lady's
gown. Old silks, velvets, and laces are in demand and the costumes are often very lovely,
especially those made for the fine Parians and
French-bisques. Old fashion magazines are at a
premium. Volumes of *Harper's Bazaar, Demo-
rest's Magazine, Peterson's Magazine,* and *Godey's
Lady's Book* have risen from fifty cents to ten
dollars, and the color plates of yesteryear are
copied for dolls of the same period. Clever wom-
en collectors find an outlet for their creative
abilities in costuming their own old dolls, and
as Mrs. Clear says, "acquire an education in the
manners, customs and dress of historic periods
that goes much deeper than anything learned at
school."

When dolls have their original clothes and

69. Dolls Costumed by Mrs. Carrie A. Hall, North Platte, Nebr.

these are not hopelessly worn, it is better not to re-dress them for clothes are evidence of age. Many dolls, however, are found without clothing, and it is amusing to dress them after looking up the suitable fashion era. Taffeta is correct for almost all periods. Old cotton or silk prints, delaines, and so on may be used. Modern taffeta is apt to cut and crack because of the fillers used, but old taffeta of the Civil War period is practically indestructible. Rayon is an anachronism for old dolls and should never be used.

Old buttons are fine to give an appearance of age to a costume. The Leghorn hats of a generation or two ago are also useful since Leghorn bonnets were much worn in the earlier periods. Delightful scoop bonnets may be created by cutting a small Milan straw hat in two and wiring it. One hat makes two bonnets. A niece of the writer makes wonderful doll bonnets from old straw hats, old cloth, and ribbons. She soaks the hats in water and reblocks them over the bottom of a round or straight-bottom jelly glass, or on a soup or tomato can, according to the size and shape desired.

Mrs. William Walker of Louisville, Kentucky, who sews for her doll collection, finds that many a seemingly hopeless old dress may be saved by lining it with net and darning the material down to the net with fine stitches.

An old-fashioned pinking iron is a useful arti-

70. Very Old Japanese Doll. Collection of Mr. and Mrs. Grant Holt, Keene, N. H.

cle for the doll dressmaker, since pinked ruffles and flounces were often used. Pinking is a term used for finishing the edges of a ruffle with tiny

71. Very Old Chinese Dolls. Collection of Mr. and Mrs. Grant Holt, Keene, N. H.

scallops. The old irons came in sets and made one-fourth-inch, three-eighths-inch, and one-half-inch scallops. They are to be found in antique shops or through advertising in mediums like the Swopper's column in *Yankee Magazine*, published at Dublin, New Hampshire. It was thus that the writer found a pinking machine which did the job by the turn of a crank. For those too young to have seen the old pinking iron in action, it may be explained that pinking was a laborious process which consisted of laying the single or folded cloth the width of the desired scallop on a hardwood block and hammering the iron down on it until the cloth was cut through. Today there are "pinking shears" but the end result is not so attractive nor so old-fashioned in appearance.

Many people also make a hobby of collecting old doll clothes, either as an end in themselves or as an adjunct to a doll collection. Where does one look for old doll clothes? One source is the dressmaker who re-dresses dolls. She almost always has a few discards on hand and will sell them reasonably, or you may buy clothes off an old doll in the hands of an "antique picker," even if you don't want to buy the doll. Antique dealers also have old doll dresses for sale at fifty cents to a dollar apiece. In short, old doll clothes, like old dolls, are just where you happen to find them.

XVII. FOR COLLECTORS

There is one bit of advice we always pass on to new collectors: DON'T LET YOUR COLLECTION GET TOO BIG. Too much becomes "clutter" about a house. Sell a few of your dolls now and then. Some weeding out will strengthen your collection and also help others. A doll you do not want may be a treasure to your neighbor. Don't be selfish! Those who have a thousand or two thousand specimens hardly know what to do with them unless they have a special room or house for dolls, such as that of Mrs. Gustave Mox of Santa Monica, California.

Fifty, a hundred, perhaps two hundred dolls are decorative in a house, and you can enjoy them more than a larger number. Select for quality rather than quantity in collecting anything, and when you acquire a doll beyond the number of your set limit, always release another to someone else. Thus you will help keep a sup-

72. *China Dolls at a National Doll Show, Charles W. Bowers Memorial Museum, Santa Ana, Calif.*

ply of dolls available and also keep prices from going too high.

A friend recently inquired, "What are you going to do with your dolls when you die? Won't you leave your collection to a museum?"

And the answer was, "Certainly not, except historical dolls. Historical dolls belong in a museum, but it's kinder to fellow collectors to let most old dolls go on the market again so that others may have the fun of collecting."

73. China Dolls at a National Doll Show, Charles W. Bowers Memorial Museum, Santa Ana, Calif.

Of course, there are some museums that need our cooperation to round out their collections as the Toy Department of the Museum of the City of New York, whose curator is Miss Janet Pinney. Here is being assembled a history of the manners and social customs of old New York as it is portrayed in the toys that were played with by her children.

Another such museum is that of the Wayne County Historical Museum at Lebanon, Ohio, where local history is being shown through dolls, as well as through other articles which belonged to early citizens.

A doll collection may also be of benefit to a community. It may be loaned to schools, libraries, and displayed in shop windows at Christmas. Doll shows may be put on to raise money for charity. Such a show was arranged by Miss Anna Dodge of Jamaica Plains, Massachusetts, and netted more than a thousand dollars for a summer camp for poor children.

An outstanding doll show is held each year from April 1 to June 15 by the Charles W. Bowers Memorial Museum at Santa Ana, California. It is under the management of Mrs. F. E. Coulter, the curator. Admission is free and the dolls are assembled by invitation from collectors all over the country. No prizes are given but each doll in the show receives a ribbon.

An important person in the doll-collecting

74. *China Dolls at a National Doll Show, Charles W. Bowers Memorial Museum, Santa Ana, Calif.*

world is invited to speak at the receptions held at the opening and the closing of the show. Some collectors cross the continent by train and by air to see the show, which brings together the rarest and finest dolls in the country. There are also collectors who make the Bowers show an annual pilgrimage. The arrangement is always artistic and beautiful for Mrs. Coulter is herself a lover of old dolls and spares no effort to make each show better than the last. One of her arrange-

75. *Dolls Displayed at a National Doll Show,
Charles W. Bowers Memorial Museum, Santa
Ana, Calif.*

ments, which has been patented, is a daguerreo-
type frame in which each doll, placed against a
suitable background, looks like a portrait. Mrs.
Coulter also uses large gilt picture frames and
places groups of dolls in little rooms with miniature furniture. For doll collectors, this show is
really worth the trip, even if you live as far away
as the East Coast.

Not many men collect dolls, but there are
good precedents. The C.I.O. leader who ran for

76. *Dolls Displayed at a National Doll Show,
Charles W. Bowers Memorial Museum, Santa
Ana, Calif.*

the office of Mayor of Detroit a few years ago has
a fine collection. A Chicago business man, a collector for forty years, selects only dolls that have
belonged to boys; a retired orthopedic surgeon
in Florida has a doll hospital where each small
"patient" has a bed of its own and wears a little
nightgown or "hospital johnnie."

Those of us, both men and women, who are

77. *Dollmaker at Work. Portrait of Lewis Sorensen of Bremerton, Wash.*

immersed in it, cannot praise too highly the hobby of doll collecting. It is an education in the dress and manners of times past; it opens new delights to the traveler and new adventures to the friendly, even if some friends are known only by their letters, or perhaps—only by their dolls.

XVIII. NATIONAL DOLL HOUSES

Krug's International Doll House, 2227 St. Paul
St., Baltimore, Md.
Antique Dolls and Modern Character Dolls.
Kimport Dolls, Independence, Mo.
Antique Dolls and Modern Character Dolls.
Just Folks Doll House, Helen Seibold Walters,
Stanton, Va.
B. H. Leffingwell, 135 Normandy Avenue, Roch-
ester, N. Y.

DOLL REPAIRS AND COSTUMING

Humpty Dumpty Doll Hospital, Redondo Beach,
Calif.
Repairs dolls except wax and papier-mâché;
supplies parts for bisque, china, and Parian
dolls; makes wigs and doll bodies; makes modern replicas of some old blonde bisques and
china dolls.

Mrs. Ralph E. Wakeman, 28 Myrtle St., Claremont, N. H.

Doll repairing of all kinds; rewaxing a specialty; expert costuming with old materials; metal hands and feet for Springfield, Vermont dolls.

Lewis Sorenson, Dollmaker, 243 South Wycoff, Bremerton, Wash.

Rewaxing.

Mrs. C. E. Hooser, Decatur, Ga.

Doll costuming.

Mrs. Carrie F. Hall, Handicraft Shop, North Platte, Nebr.

Costumes, and makes modern portrait dolls.

NOTE: Old dolls are where you find them— attics, antique shops and booths in various antique shows.

XIX. TERMS USED IN DOLL COLLECTING

"Biedermeier" China-Head. Smooth head with a black tonsurelike spot to which a wig was attached. The Biedermeier period (1815–1850) was one of simplicity in German art and furniture.

Bisque. Term applied to pottery and other earthenware finished in one firing and not intended to be glazed.

Blonde-Bisque Heads. Unglazed clay heads, delicately tinted. (Cf. *Parian heads,* which are untinted.)

Bonnet Dolls. Usually stone-bisque (sometimes wax) heads with molded hats or bonnets.

Bru Dolls. French bisque dolls manufactured by M. Bru, contemporary of M. Jumeau. Heavier features and darker coloring than Jumeaus.

Character Dolls. Bisque or composition dolls of genre type, representing well-known persons such as Sonja Henie, Shirley Temple, the Dionne quintuplets.

China-Head Dolls. Heads made of white clay, tinted, fired, dipped in glaze, and refired.

Composition Dolls. Dolls made in Germany of a combination of wood flour, starch, and rosin mixed with water. Had wigs. (There was also a French type made with painted hair.)

Dresden. Term applied to some glazed china heads with the crossed-swords mark of the

Dresden factories under the glaze on the back of the left shoulder. These heads should not be confused with the Parian *unglazed* heads which are also called Dresden.

Fabric Dolls. Made of cloth or felt—rag dolls, Lenci felt, Ravaca, Kathe Kruse dolls. Also those made of cotton sheets issued by commercial houses as advertisements.

"Flirting-Eye" Dolls. Bisque papier-mâché, or German, from about 1850 on. Eyes move from side to side, not up and down.

French-Bisque. Blonde-bisque heads made in France, primarily at the Jumeau factory.

French-Fashion Dolls. Bisque dolls made in the late nineteenth century, particularly by Jumeau and Bru, with elaborate clothes to show fashions, as Milliners' Models did in early part of century.

"Frozen Charlottes." Small jointless bisque and china dolls.

German-Bisque. Highly colored bisque heads made in Germany.

Godey-Head. China-head doll, blonde or brunette, with molded headdress of vertical pointed curls.

Greiner. German dollmaker who took out the first American patent for dolls in 1858. Worked in Philadelphia.

Greiner Dolls. Papier-mâché heads, blonde and brunette, with cloth reinforcements. *Painted* eyes.

Joel Ellis Dolls. Jointed wooden type with mortise and tenon joints made in Springfield, Vermont.

Jumeau Dolls. Blonde-bisque dolls made in France by the Jumeaus from about 1862 until about 1898. Blown-glass eyes. Fourteen sizes. After 1869, swivel necks, jointed wooden bodies, and other improvements. Finally composition body strung with elastic.

M. & S. Superior Dolls. A type of composition doll. Maker unknown. Large or small, blonde or brunette. Labeled. Commercial body of cloth stuffed with hair.

Milliners' Models. Early nineteenth-century dolls, 5 to 26 inches long, with papier-mâché heads, unjointed kid bodies, and wooden arms and legs. Used to carry new fashions before the era of fashion magazines.

Montanari Dolls. Thick wax dolls without reinforcement. Made in England. Each hair set directly in wax with hot needle. No wigs.

Name Dolls. China heads made in Germany, after 1898, with girls' names—Helen, Ethel, etc.—embossed in the china and painted gold.

Papier-Mâché. Macerated paper, cooked, mixed with glue. First used for doll heads about 1820.

Parian or Dresden Dolls. Probably from Dresden factories in Germany, of very fine unglazed clay, originally white like Parian marble—hence the name. Beautifully modeled. More often blonde than brunette. Painted or blown-glass eyes. (Parians *by usage* include blonde-bisques.)

Peddler Dolls. Of carved wood and carrying a basket containing numerous miniature articles.

Portrait Dolls. Dolls supposedly representing famous persons—Queen Victoria, Jenny Lind, Countess Dagmar, etc.

Pre-Greiner Dolls. Large, with papier-mâché heads and *blown glass* eyes, made in Germany from about 1830 to 1845.

"Pumpkin-Head" Dolls. Wax heads with molded pompadours with a band like a circular comb around the head. Dark glass eyes but no pupils.

Schoenhut Dolls. Wooden dolls made in Philadelphia from 1911 to 1924.

Springfield Dolls. Wooden dolls made in Springfield, Vermont, by Joel Ellis and Mason & Taylor from 1873 to about 1885.

"Squash-Head" Dolls. See "Pumpkin-Head" Dolls.

Stone-Bisque. Coarse type of unglazed clay head, similar to finer Parian or blonde-bisque heads.

Wax Dolls. Various types of thick wax heads or papier-mâché heads, dipped in wax. Types vary according to the time and the manufacturer.

Wire-Eyed. Wax dolls with sleeping eyes manipulated by a wire at the waist, instead of counterweights.

INDEX

Italic numbers refer to illustrations.